Sacred Classics

On the recordings:
 * Ida Huber, soprano
 ** Kenneth Bozeman, tenor
    Bill Casey, piano
    Recorded August 1991, Milwaukee; Richard Walters, producer

To access companion recorded performances
and accompaniments online, visit:
www.halleonard.com/mylibrary

Enter Code
3282-6715-3309-0628

On the cover: El Greco, *The Miracle of Christ Healing the Blind*, Oil on canvas, 47 x 57 1/2 in.,
The Metropolitan Museum of Art

ISBN: 978-0-7935-6659-4

HAL•LEONARD® CORPORATION
7777 W. BLUEMOUND RD. P.O. BOX 13819 MILWAUKEE, WI 53213

Visit Hal Leonard Online at
www.halleonard.com

Dank sei Dir, Herr

(Thanks Be to God)

Siegfried Ochs*
(Previously attributed to Handel)

*Siegfried Ochs (1858-1929) claimed to have discovered an aria by Handel, and to have made an arrangement of the piece, which was published and became well-known. Closer research has revealed that this is actually an original composition by Ochs.

- ra - el hin durch das Meer.
grate - ful thanks be to Thee.

con espressione

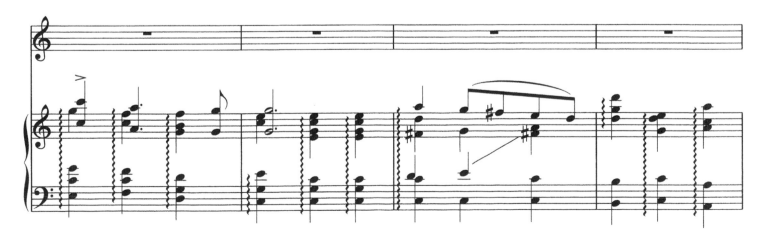

sempre **f**
pp

Wie ei - ne Her - de zog es hin - durch,
Like a great flock Thy hand ev - er led us,

p
p

Herr, Dei - ne Hand Schütz - te es,
Lord Thy hand leads us,

in Dei - ner Gü - te gabst Du ihm Heil.
By all Thy good - ness Sal - va - tion is ours.

mf

Dank _____
Thanks _____

_ sei Dir, { Dank _____
_ be to God, { Herr, _____ sei Dir,
opt. { Dank _____ be to
Thanks _____

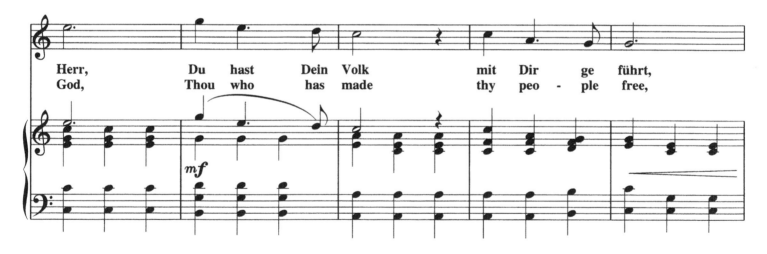

Herr, Du hast Dein Volk mit Dir ge führt,
God, Thou who has made thy peo - ple free,

Is - ra - el hin durch das Meer.
All grate - ful thanks be to Thee.

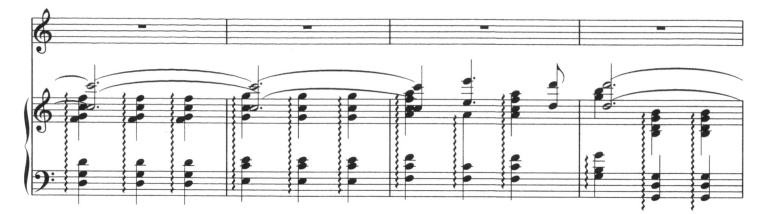

sempre forte

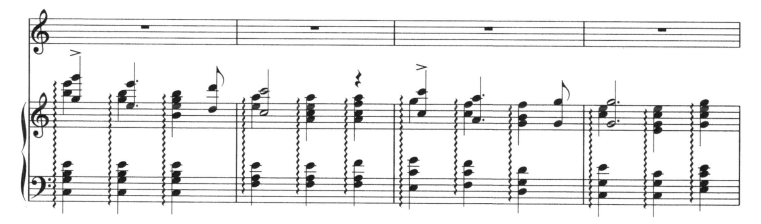

ff

Panis Angelicus

César Franck

Pa - nis an -

ge - li-cus fit pa - nis ho - mi-num,

Dat pa - nis coe - li-cus fi - gu - ris ter - mi -

num. O res mi - ra - bi -lis

man - du - cat Do - mi-num, Pau - per,

pau - per, ser - vus et hu - mi - lis,

Pau - per, pau - per, ser - vus et hu - mi -

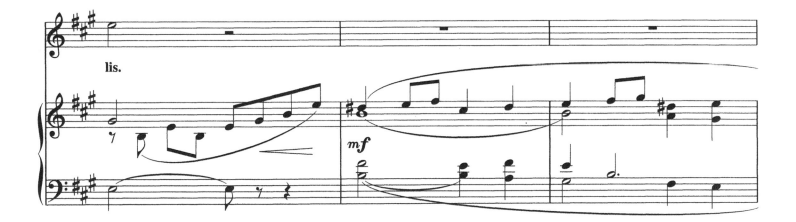

lis.

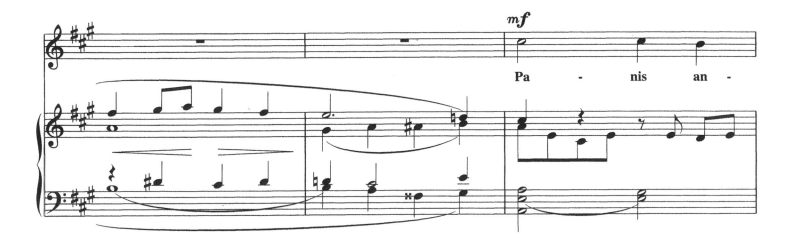

Pa - nis an -

ge - li-cus   fit   pa - nis   ho - mi-num,

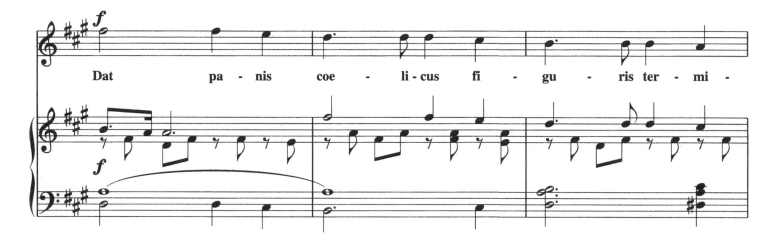

Dat   pa - nis   coe - li-cus   fi - gu - ris   ter - mi -

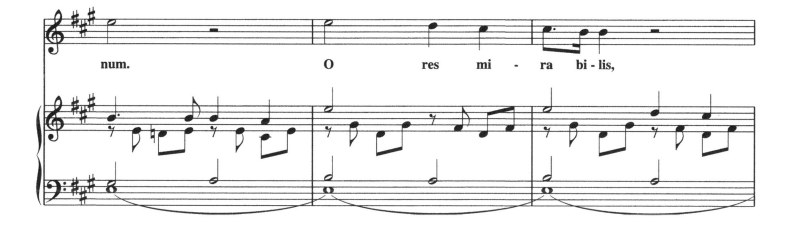

num.   O   res   mi - ra   bi - lis,

man - du - cat   Do - mi-num   Pau - per, __

pau - per, ser - vus et hu - mi - lis,

Pau - per, _ pau - per, ser - vus, _ ser - vus et

hu - mi - lis.

decresc.

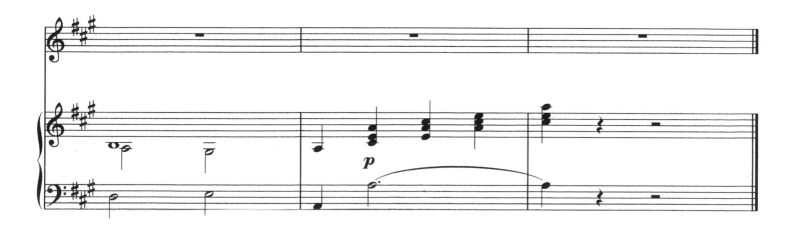

p

Ave Maria
(adapted from "Prelude in C" by J.S. Bach)

Charles Gounod

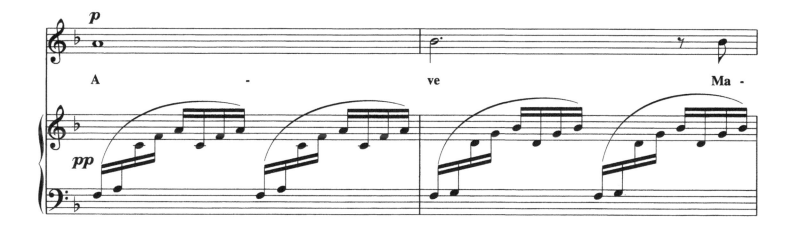

The full performance on the CD is up a whole-step, in G Major. The accompaniment track is in the printed key of F Major.

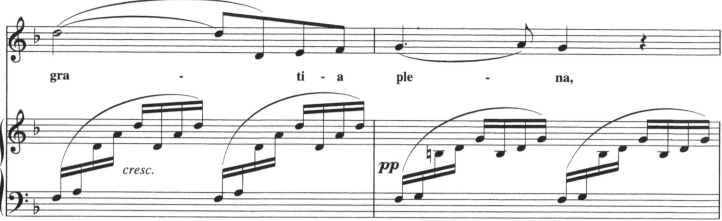

gra - ti - a ple - na,

Do - mi - nus te - cum.

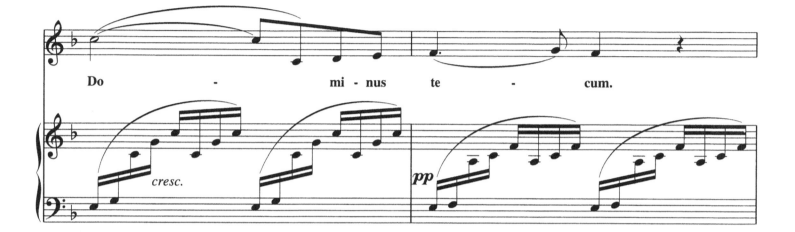

be - ne - dic - ta

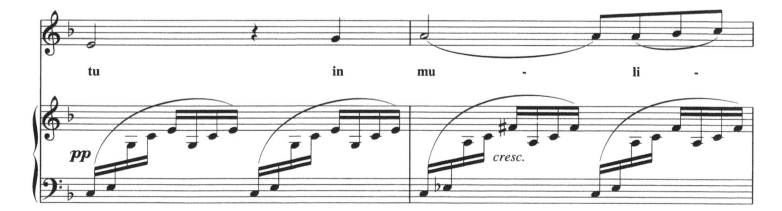

tu in mu - li -

e - ri - bus et _____ be - ne -

dic - tus fruc - tus_____

ven - tris _____ tu - i Je -

sus. _____ Sanc - ta Ma -

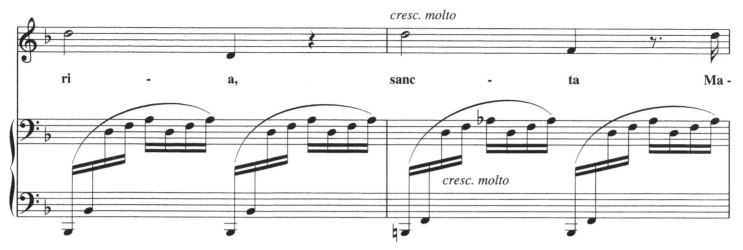

nunc _____ et ___ in ho - ra, in

ho - ra ___ mor - tis ___ nos - trae, ___

A - men!

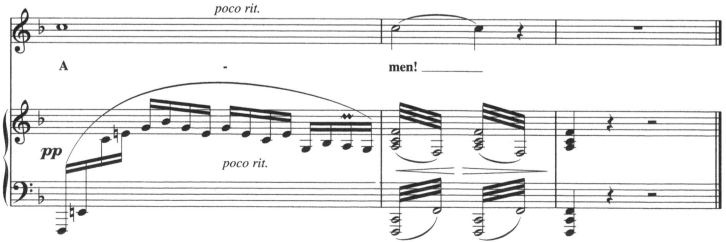

A - men! _____

Agnus Dei
(Lamb of God)

Georges Bizet

dolce espressivo

A - gnus De - i! qui tol - lis pec - ca - ta

mun - di, mi - se - re - re, mi - se -

re - re no - bis. A - gnus

De - i! qui ___ tol - lis pec - ca - ta mun - di,

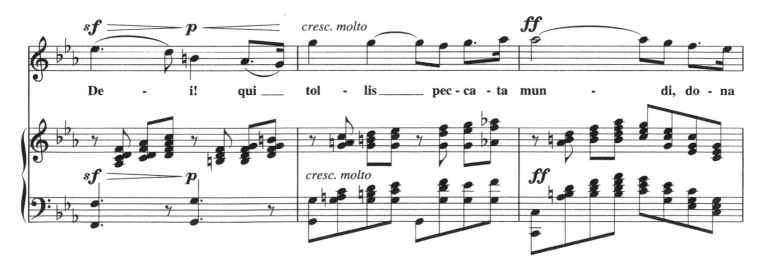

O Divine Redeemer
(Repentir)

Charles Gounod

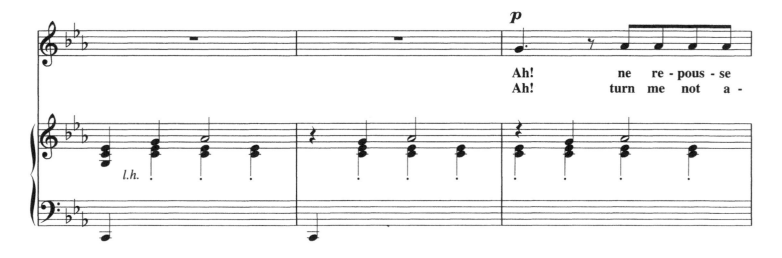

Ah!   ne re - pous - se
Ah!   turn me not a -

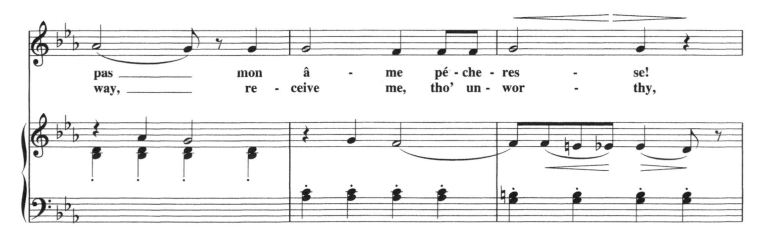

pas _____ mon â - me pé - che - res - se!
way, _____ re - ceive me, tho' un - wor - thy,

Ah! ne re - pous - se pas _____ mon à - me pé - che -
Ah! turn me not a - way, _____ re - ceive me, tho' un -

res - se! En - tends mes cris, en - tends mes cris et
wor - thy! Hear Thou my cry, en hear Thou my cry, be -

vois mon re - pen - tir! À mon ai - de, Sei -
hold, Lord, my dis - tress! An-swer me from thy

gneur, _____ hâ - te - toi d'ac-cou - rir, et prends pi -
throne. _____ haste Thee, Lord, to mine aid, Thy pit - y

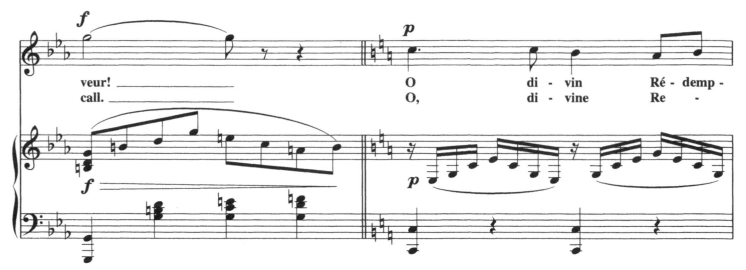

veur! _____ O di - vin Ré - demp-
call. _____ O, di - vine Re -

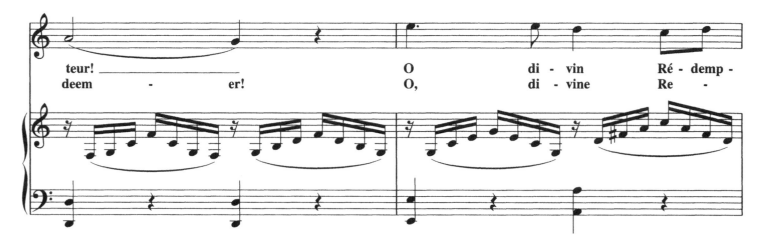

teur! _____ O di - vin Ré - demp-
deem - er! O, di - vine Re -

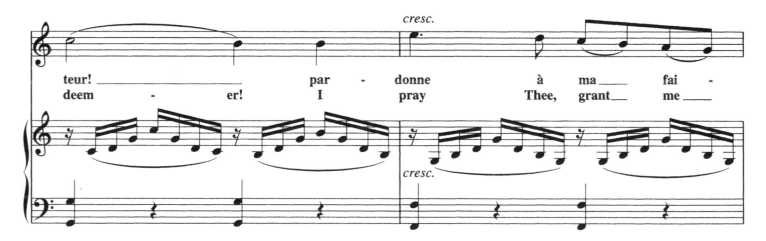

teur! _____ par - donne à ma ___ fai -
deem - er! I pray Thee, grant ___ me ___

bles - se, ___ par - don - ne, par - donne á ma fai -
par - don, ___ and re - mem - ber not, re - mem - ber not my

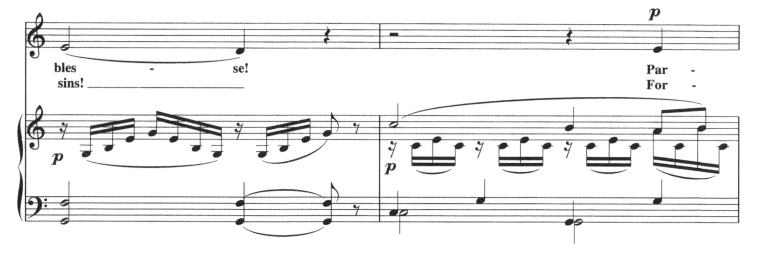

bles - se! Par -
sins! _____ For -

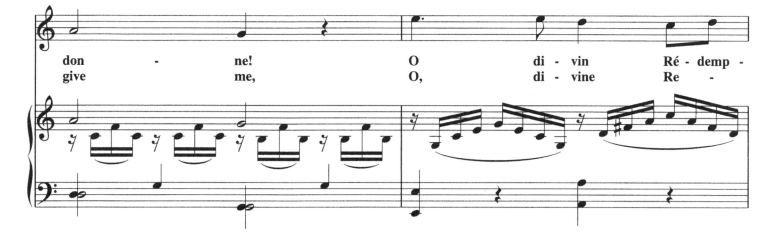

don - ne! O di - vin Ré - demp -
give me, O, di - vine Re -

teur! _____ par - donne à ma ___ fai -
deem - er! I pray Thee, grant ___ me ___

bles - se, ___ par - don - ne, par - donne à ma fai -
par - don, ___ and re - mem - ber not, re - mem - ber not, O

cresc.

al - té - ré _____ du sang - lant sa - cri -
hear my cry! _____ Save me, Lord, in Thy

fi - ce, bé - ni - ra _____
mer - cy; hear my cry, _____

_ de ta main les clé - men - tes ri - gueurs! _
_ hear my cry! Come and save me, O Lord! _

O di - vin Ré - demp - teur! _____
O, di - vine Re - deem - er!

O   di - vin   Ré - demp - teur! _____ par -
O,   di - vine   Re - deem - er! ___ I

donne   à ma___ fai - bles - se, ___ par -
pray   Thee, grant ___ me ___ par - don ___ and re -

don - ne, par - donne à ma fai - bles -
mem - ber not, re - mem - ber not, O Lord,   my

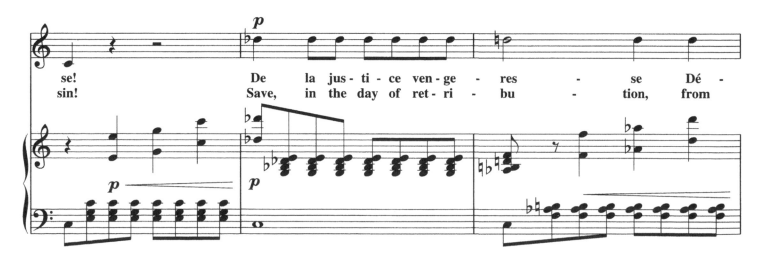

se!   De la jus - ti - ce ven - ge - res - se Dé -
sin!   Save, in the day of ret - ri - bu - tion, from

cresc.

tour - ne les coups, mon Sau - veur!   O   di - vin Ré - demp-
Death shield Thou me,   O my God!   O,   di - vine Re -

poco rit.

teur! _____ par - don - ne
deem - er, have mer - cy!

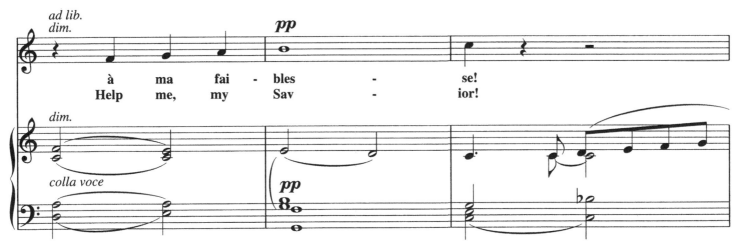

ad lib.
dim.   *pp*

à ma fai - bles - se!
Help me, my Sav - ior!

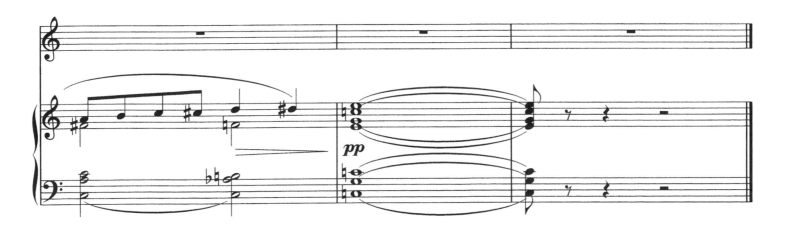

The Palms
(Les Rameaux)

Jean-Baptiste Faure

Andante maestoso

O'er all the way, green palms and
Sur nos che-mins les ra - meaux

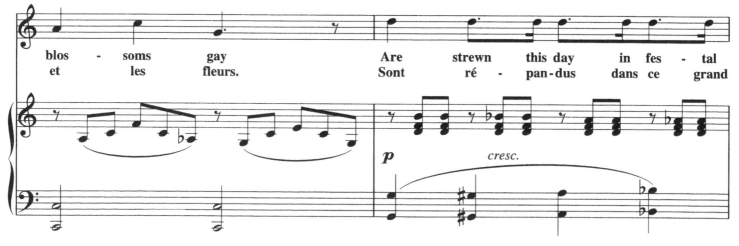

blos - soms gay. Are strewn this day in fes - tal
et les gay fleurs. Sont ré - pan - dus dans ce grand

pre - - - par - a - tion; Where Je - sus comes to wipe our
jour _____ de fê - - te, Jé - sus s'a - van - ce, il vient sé -

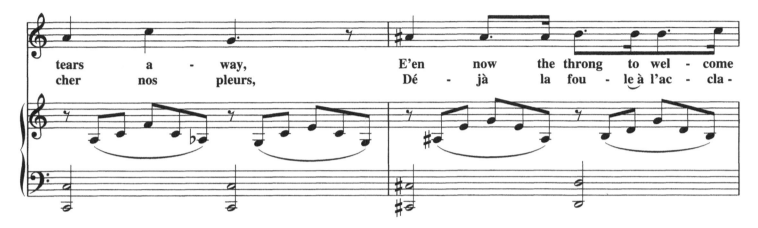

tears a - way, E'en now the throng to wel - come
cher nos pleurs, Dé - jà la fou - le à l'ac - cla -

rall. *a tempo*

Him pre - pare; Join all and sing, _____ His
mer s'ap - prête; Peu - ples, chan - tez, _____ chan -

ff *rall.* *mf* *a tempo*

name _____ de-clare Let ev - 'ry voice re - sound in
tez _____ en chœur, Que vo - tre voix á no - tre

p

ac - - cla - ma - - tion. Ho - san - - na!
voix ____ ré - pon - de. Ho - san - - na!

Praise ye the Lord! Bless Him who com-eth to bring us sal -
Gloi - re au Sei-gneur! Bé - ni ce - lui qui vient sau-ver le

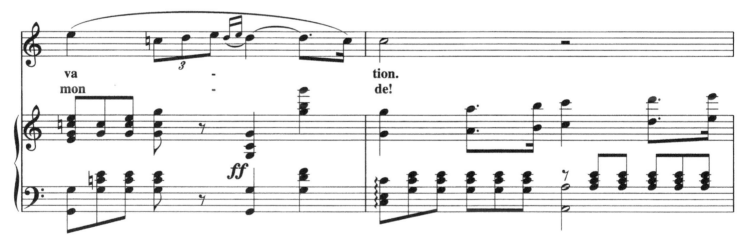

va - - tion.
mon - de!

His word goes forth, and peo-ples by its might
Il a par-lé, les peu-ples à sa voix
Sing and re-joice, O blest Je-ru-sa-lem,
Ré - jou-is-toi, Sain-te Jé-ru-sa-lem,

Once more re-gain free-dom from de - gra-da - tion,
Ont re-cou-vré leur li-ber-té per-du - e,
Of all Thy sons sing the e-man - ci-pa - tion.
De tes en-fants chan-te la dé - li-vran - ce;

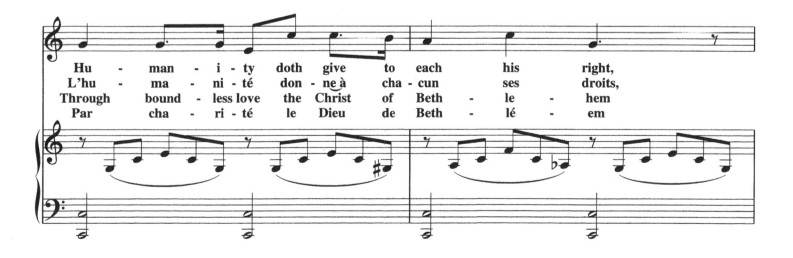

Hu - man - i-ty doth give to each his right,
L'hu - ma-ni-té don-ne à cha-cun ses droits,
Through bound-less love the Christ of Beth-le - hem
Par cha-ri-té le Dieu de Beth-lé - em

While those in dark - ness find re - stored the light.
Et la lu - miè - re est à cha - cun ren - due;
Brings faith and hope to Thee for ev - er - more
A - vec la foi t'ap - por - te l'es - pé - rance!

Join all and sing,_____ His name_____ de - clare,
Peu - ples, chan - tez,_____ chan - tez_____ en chœur,

Let ev 'ry voice re - sound with ac - cla - ma - tion. Ho -
Que vo - tre voix á no - tre voix_____ ré - pon - de. Ho -

san - na! Praise ye the Lord!
san - na! Gloi - re au Sei - gneur!

Bless Him who com-eth to bring us sal va - tion!
Bé - ni ce - lui qui vient sau - ver le mon - de!

Optional high notes are for the final verse.

Crucifixus

Jean-Baptiste Faure

rez, _____ ve - nez à ce Dieu: car il pleu - re, Vous qui souf-
Him, _____ all ye who weep; for He too weep eth. Come un - to

frez, ve - nez à lui: car il gué rit.
Him, all ye who mourn; for He can heal.

Vous qui trem - blez, ve - nez à
Come un - to Him, all ye who

lui, _____ ve - nez à lui: _____ car
fear, _____ Come _____ un - to Him, _____ in

il _____ sou - rit. **Vous qui pas -**
woe _____ and weal. *Come un - to*

sez, ve - nez à lui: car il de meu - re, car il de -
Him, in your last sleep; He nev - er sleep - eth, He nev - er

meu - re. **Vous qui pas - sez, ve -**
sleep - eth. Come un - to Him, in

nez à lui: car il de - meu - re. **Vous qui pas -**
your last sleep; He nev - er sleep - eth. Come un - to

The Holy City

F. E. Weatherly and Stephen Adams

Last night I lay a-sleep-ing There came a dream so fair. I
then me-thought my dream was changed, the streets no long - er rang.

stood in old Je - ru - sa - lem, Be - side the tem - ple there; I
Hushed were the glad Ho - san - nas The lit - tle child - ren sang; The

heard the child - ren sing - ing, And ev - er as they sang, Me -
sun grew dark with mys - ter - y, The morn was cold and chill As the

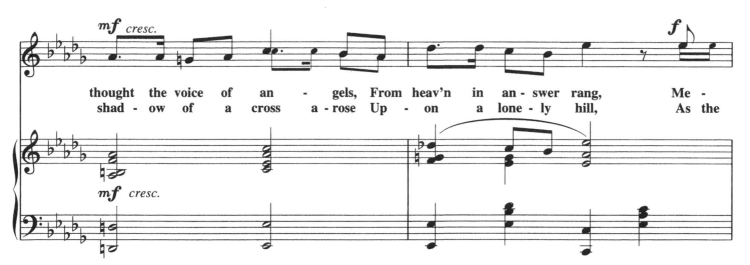

thought the voice of an - gels, From heav'n in an - swer rang, Me -
shad - ow of a cross a - rose Up - on a lone - ly hill, As the

thought the voice of an - gels From
shad - ow of a cross a - rose Up -

heav'n in an - swer rang. Je -
on a lone - ly hill. Je -

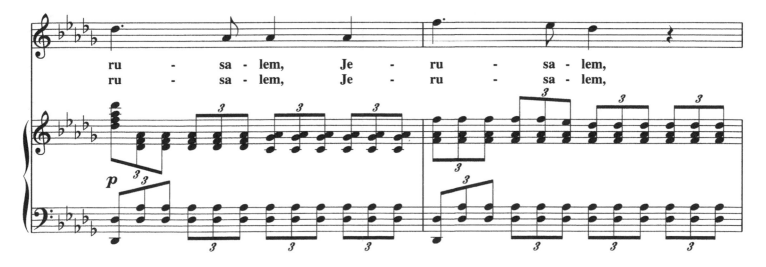

ru - sa - lem, Je - ru - sa - lem,
ru - sa - lem, Je - ru - sa - lem,

Lift up your gates and sing,
Hark how the an - gels sing,
Ho -

san - na in the high - est, Ho -

san - na to your King!

And

no one was de - nied. No

need of moon or stars by night, Or

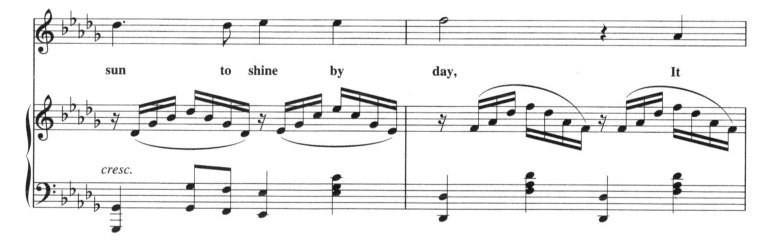

sun to shine by day, It

was the new Je - ru - sa - lem That

would not pass a - way. It

was the new Je - ru - sa - lem That would not pass a -

way. Je - ru - sa - lem, Je -

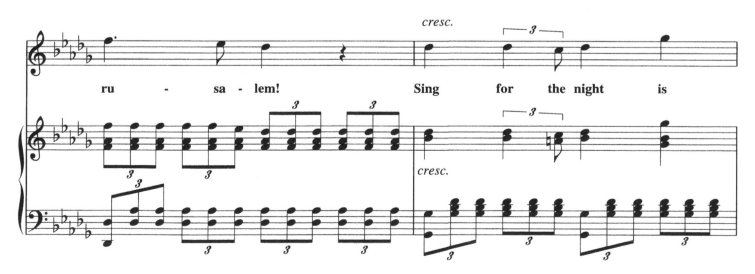

ru - sa - lem! Sing for the night is

o'er! Ho - san - na in __ the high - est, Ho -

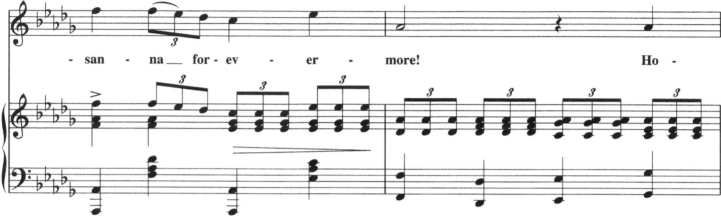

- san - na __ for - ev - er - more! Ho -

san - na in the high - est, __ Ho - san - na __ for ev - er -

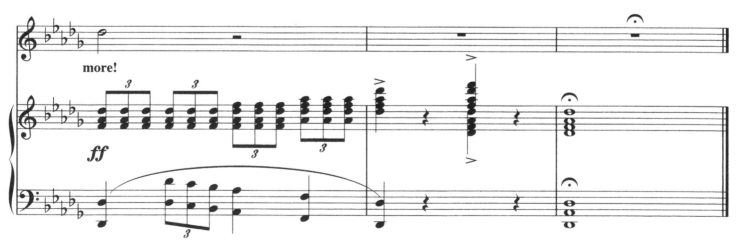

more!

Hear My Prayer, O Lord

Antonín Dvořák

48

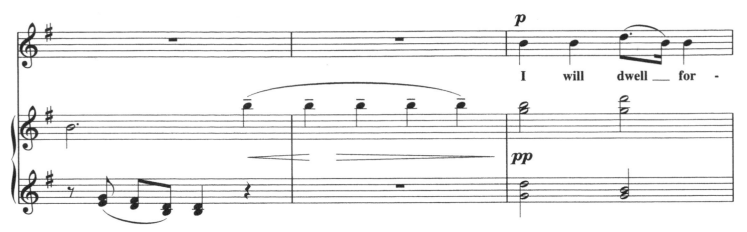

I will dwell ___ for -

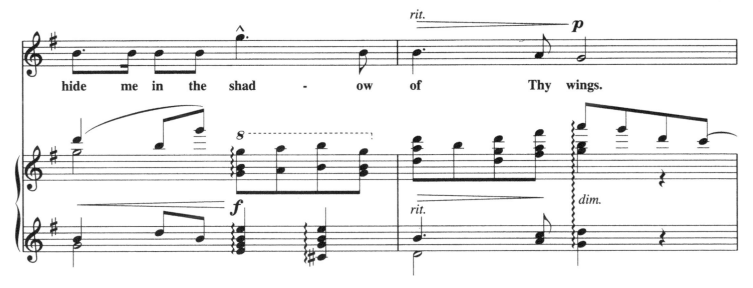

ev - er in Thy tents ___ and

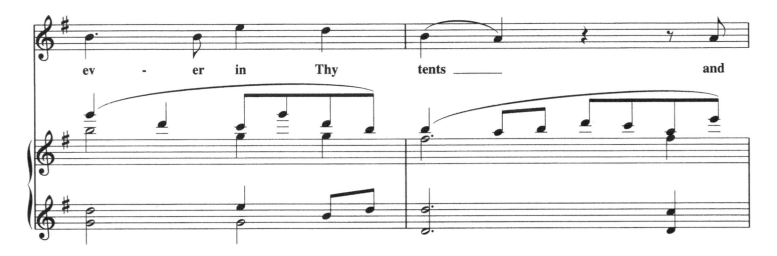

rit. *p*

hide me in the shad - ow of Thy wings.

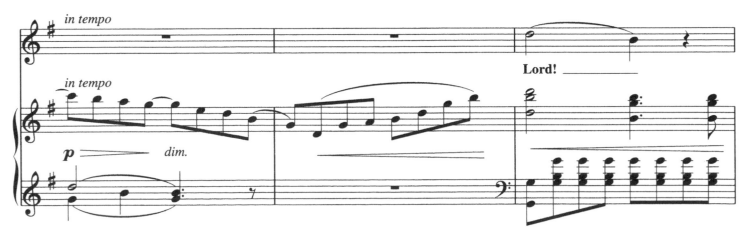

in tempo

Lord! ___

Thou art in - deed my God, yea, I will seek Thee

ear - ly. My soul is faint, my bod - y long - eth,

long - eth af - ter Thee

in a bar - ren de - sert where there is no wa - ter.

Now I will bless Thee

dai - ly and lift my hands in pray'r and ad - o - ra - tion;

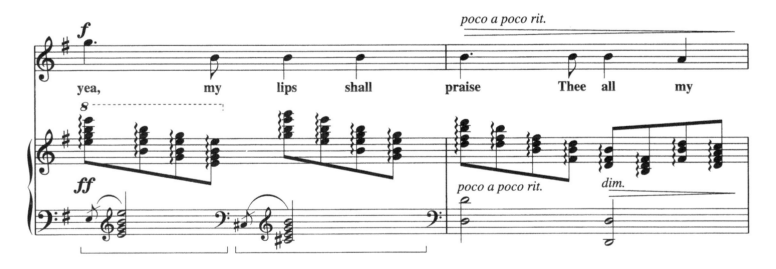

poco a poco rit.

yea, my lips shall praise Thee all my

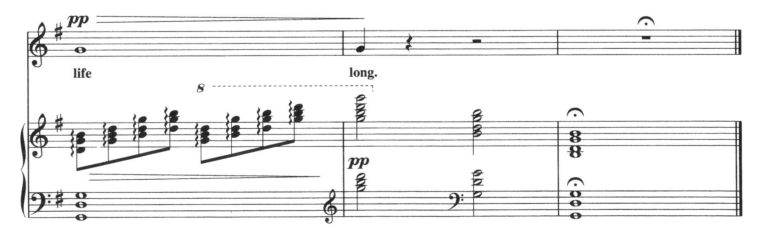

life long.

I Will Sing New Songs

Antonín Dvořák

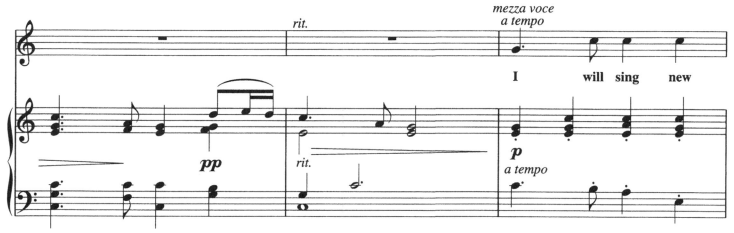

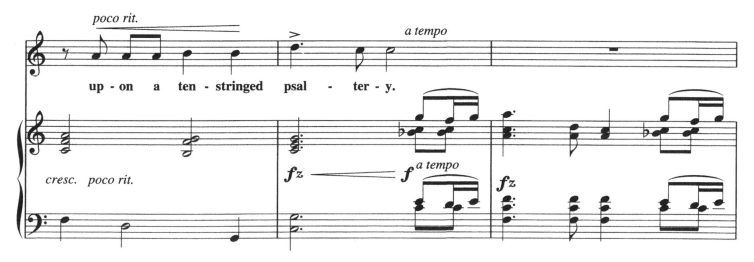

Ev - 'ry day will I ex - tol Thee

and will bless Thy Ho - ly Name, ____

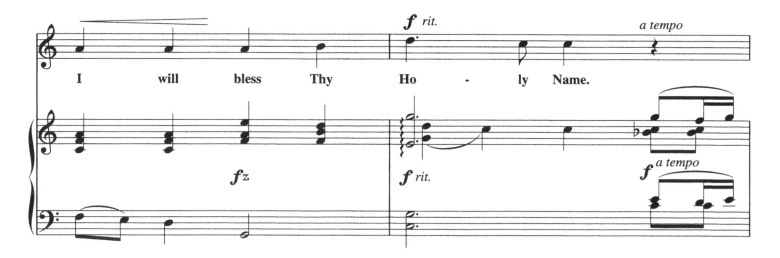

I will bless Thy Ho - ly Name.

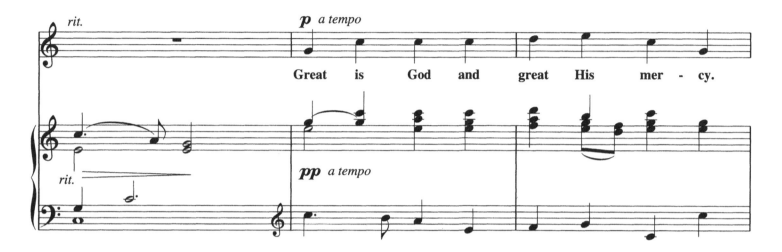

Great is God and great His mer - cy.

Who shall tell of all His great - ness? Who shall His

pow'r de-clare?

My song shall be of praise and hon - or, and of Thy glo - rious

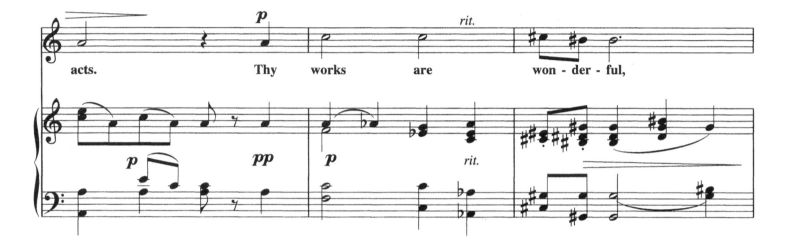

acts. Thy works are won - der - ful, past our know - ing.

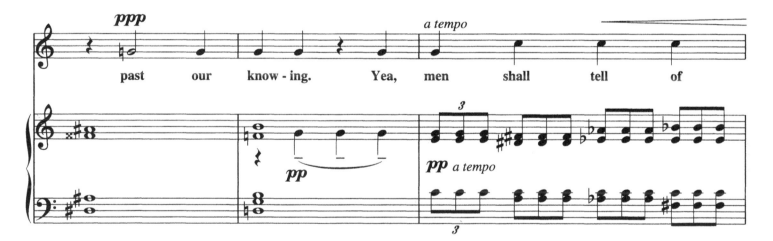

Yea, men shall tell of

Thy great kind - ness and of Thy won - d'rous

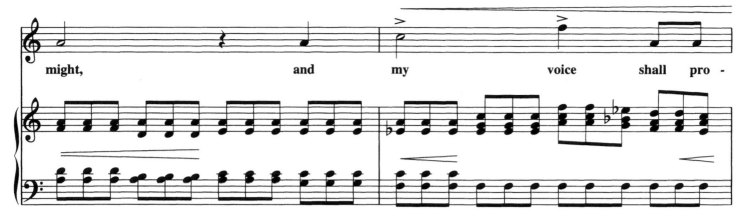

might, and my voice shall pro -

claim a - loud Thy glo - ry.

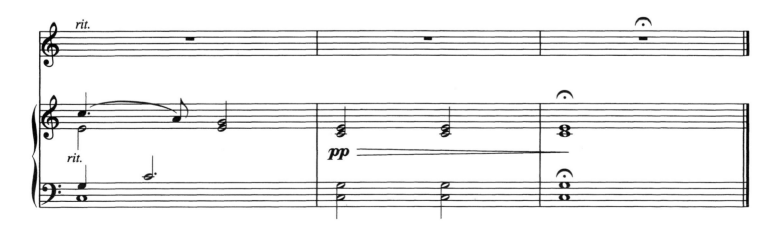